WORDS FROM THE HOUSE OF THE DEAD
Prison Writings From Soledad

A FACSIMILE VERSION OF A BOOK
6:15 Unlock—A Kite From Soledad
HANDMADE BY PRISONERS & SMUGGLED OUT

With Introductions by Joseph Bruchac & William Witherup
And a Glossary of Joint Jargon
And additional prison material marked off by borders

A Note From Technical Advisor, Paul Glover:

Their imagination has not been greyed. From within a grey world these prisoners affirm that, within this book, their playful, bright, and inventive spirit is unbeaten and unregulated. Color is essential to closer appreciation of their feeling. In the original book, color is their expressive tool almost as much as alphabet. We cannot replicate such color, but only acknowledge it.

The jetplane flies orange against numerous blues.
The world, on the last page, is realistically ruddy-cheeked. brown and blue, sucking the green stem of an S below a red afterward and above a moon in orange slice aspect.
The hatbatcatvat story proceeds through a crayola forest.
The recurring brickwork pattern is blue, and the boldface red.
Purple and yellow embrace Yin Yang together.
Leafy blotches are pressed on from watercolor-soaked flora.
There are real flowers faded to pastels, real feathers, real paper dolls, passes, cards, and color photo.

In some instances, because of the color, clear black and white prints could not be produced. I tried to reclaim these missing or fragmented sections by hand, with a dedication to the original.

 THE CROSSING PRESS, Trumansburg, New York 14886

The Crossing Press Series of Contemporary Anthologies

Copyright 1974 The Crossing Press
SBN 912278-47-1, paper
SBN 912278-46-3, cloth
LC 73-86672

2nd Enlarged Edition
First Edition published by The Greenfield Review Press, 1971

Maria Gonzales
1445 W 45th
Fresno Calif

Correctional Training Fac.
Soledad Calif.

To Whom It May Concern:

The reason I'm writing this letter is because I'd like to know of what or how does things go about, when a inmate makes things then, sent home and don't recieve them?

In my case what happen was that my husband Roberto Gonzales (B 22492) had sent home wallets and hairpins and I didn't recieve them. He has wrote and told me I should of recieved them. It's been past thirty days and still I haven't received them. Should it take long to recieve a package?

I hope I can hear from you and more or less know of what could have happen. I thank you for taking the time and consideration on my letter.

sincerely, M. Gonzales.

DEAR MARIA, MAY IT CONCERN US

FROM THE BOWELS OF THE MOTHERFUCKING MACHINE

THE 6:15 UNLOCK

A KITE FROM SOLEDAD

Books By the Same Authors

The Lost Train
How To Write Hiply
Leaves of Corpus
Collected Blues, Rocks, Letters
and Poems

I shortened Stories
Barely Collected
but Alive.

II Poems unpretty - but
Also Alive

WHERE THE PLANET GROWS HIGH
- a complete guide to organic
hallucinogens of North America ~

WORRABLEEHW ETIHW YM DNIM
!UOY LLIW ,ESUOHERAW

also!

SOLEDAD VALEDICTORIAN, A speech

A.U.M. (the meaning of the name)

PREFACE

a haggard group of busted
travelers met by chance in
the scandal-ridden soledad
penitentary in california.
when they clicked just like
a downtown ruckus it was
clear that the subjective
aspect of the famous SOLEDAD
INVESTIGATIONS would have to
be done by volunteers.

understaffed and without
sleep, reward or thoughts
of recognition, our humble
researchers, compilers and
investigators toiled and
assembled the enclosed
report in book form.

it is hoped that eventually
the work will be made avail-
able to every university in
america and to every place
where concerned citizens go
to gather. it is hoped also
and too, that the work will
come to be regarded as a
standard reference work in
the field of penology as it
offers a brillant portrayal
and an up-to-date view of the
criminal mind in the prisons
of amerika, and as such,
should not be regarded as an
attempt at artistic art, but
rather as social art which
thoroughly acquaints society
and the citizens thereof with
the criminal...

october 1970

willhelm washington

as i write this ⊃

INTRODUCTION

the afternoon stretches, warm
bright, peacefully around me.
Just below my bare feet flows
the Danube, beginning to
look blue once more in all
but the spring freshets, when
gobs of plastic shit and swirls
of vile yellow scum come vomiting
down. This season she runs clear
again, we've started to drink her water.
From around the
bend come exited voices of blue-
jays, joined by the sounds of my
son and his friends, and mixed
with fragrance of fresh wood;
they're hewing willows, building
a small waterwheel. . . .
Near me lies this
book, just now the landingstrip

for a butterfly. Memories come by, of the times these poems were written, so long ago in feeling, yet so close when measured by the planet's leaps around the sun. . . .

Memories of the last days of the concrete and computer age, already becoming a legend, growing clearer with distance and the birth of each new human here.

At Nights, in the Kivas and the long houses, you can hear the troubadours sing ballads. Ballads of how the global systems of technocratic authoritarianism and legal greed collapsed just after the return of the last manned moon mission.

-Soyex 14 i believe it was called.-
Of how the awe-
some, allpower, all brain, mile-
cubed, plugged-in god of the
ministry of control, information
and conformity ordered all
media off, when a container
of rare moondust went missing,
shortly after splashdown....
Of how it was
discovered that even a pinch
of this moondust, mixed with Coca-
Cola, has the mysterious, joyous
property of turning concrete
into fertile bullshit... Elimina-
ting the need for explosives.
How freeways
changed into verdant trails,
cities into lush gardens, prisons
into compost piles....

Now here and there, men and women, with many forced into a freak monastic experience, felt themselves no longer able to suppress their nature, nor willing to act according to the twisted conditioning taught and demanded by the rational murderous insanity of those days.

Now, following the trail of Korzybski and Reich, the call of Leary, the magic of Tolkien and Vonnegut and Brautigan, the strategy of Krishnamurti, the music of "them", and the beatles and dylan, they began to flow toward that vortex of clarity: Where "Energy Is"

It is my pleasure to now pass around this bundle of songs and inspired cries, from men who refused to be named, who would be neither heroes, nor martyrs, nor leaders, who intuitively sought to abandon their pain with their desires.

They took the tools at hand. Defying the death machine, which had modified the dragon's teeth, and filed them into nihilistic abstractions for justifying its headlong rush into the apocalypse, together they defanged the dragon, each withdrawing his energy, his unique manifestation of the life force. Together they restrung its teeth, into radiant, rhythmic, harmonious leis.

They also were among the first to understand the need for intuitive matriarchy as our socially guiding principl

Read them, shiver with them in pain; sing with them of the dawn of our times & be warmed again and again by their hope, a hope based on certainty.

When the seed of now sprouted in the chaos of then....

Vienna, summer 1979

Knut Hans Jacobsen
(still at the music
convention!)

Let the slave, grinding at the mill,
   run out into the field,
Let him look up into the heavens
   & laugh in the bright air.
Let the inchained soul, shut up in
   darkness and in sighing,
Whose face has never seen a smile
   in thirty weary years,
Rise and look out, his chains are loose,
   his dungeon doors are open;
And let his wife and children return
   from the oppressor's scourge.

   (Blake, from the four zoas)

We come,
we come with roll of drum:
ta-runda runda runda rom!

6:15 UNLOCK

REVEILLE! REVEILLE! blinding lights/scream-
ing bells/agony accellerates/drips of the
barf coloured walls/ six inches concrete in
all directions/get up/clean cell/prisoner/
RELEASE FOR EARLY CHOW AND DIET LINE!
shitters flush/doors slam/clomp down the
tier/the steel stairs/past first watch guard/
end of his shift/guarding prisoners/onto the
mainline/feedline shuffle/100 prisoners long/
step bread/step porridge/step two grams oleo/
step etc./tin tray tin cup/racket/hurry up/
feed 1200/ in 37 minutes/almighty schedule/
SICK CALL! SICK CALL! to dull the pain/
another line/wait/tell your shuck to the
m.t.a./he's heard them all/500 aspirins
later/lie in your cell/wish today cancelled/
RELEASE LAUNDRY AND CULINARY WORKERS ONLY!
inmates run the facility/prisoners are
forced to keep their prison/obey the rules/
THERE WILL BE NO BODY AND FENDER TODAY!
PREPARE TO RELEASE INDUSTRIES AND MAINTE=
NANCE CREWS ONLY! half a mile main line/
institution squats in the valley as a
cancerous scorpion/maen/east gate lineup/
hey home where you been/the motherfuckers
threw me in the hole/peanutbutter with a
prior/stripcell/29 day program/a.c./
PREPARE TO RELEASE VOCATIONAL SCHOOL! THERE
WILL BE NO BODY AND FENDER TODAY! cellblock e
closed down/chican murdered a white canteen
punk/stabbed 47 times/with his own piece/
his ticket came with him from quentin/
PREPARE TO RELEASE ACADEMIC SCHOOL! get out
of my face/shorttimer/shit i could do six
months standing on my head/swing cellkey/
PREPARE TO RELEASE FOR THE YARD! punishment
for guards/manning the 10 machine guns/in the
10 phallic guard towers/hards on/barbwire
fence/triple galvanised/permanent/ unobstruc-
ted view in every direction/out of bounds/
hit the fence/shoot escapees on sight/
PREPARE TO RELEASE LAUNDRY CARTS AND DUCATS!
a regular/all bonaroo/with all 5 beef for
nuisance contraband/ the disciplinary com-

ittee/they'll take your date/hot dog and
hank books/on record in your jacket/
OFFICER SMITH CALL 263! jive assed fish/
armored machine/bright badge/keys jang-
ling/$500 per month/mortgage/black boots/
paranoid/just following orders/car pay-
ments in the parking lot/allamerikaboy/
**A 29498 ELDRIDGE CLEAVER REPORT TO THE
EAST GATE!** 1400 souls on ice here/20
more prisons within 100 miles/babylon/
CLEAR THE CORRIDOR, CLEAR THE CORRIDOR!
investigation/present shiny image/corr-
ectional training facility for men/no-
thing to hide/the program/i.w.f./10%/
YARD UNLOCK! jockers and their broads/
flip flop punks/wing porters/if you got
juice/buff to the hub on the ironpile/
got big/lowrider hands you a wolfticket/
jam you/jack you up/down your shit/kid/
**THE FOLLOWING MEN WILL REPORT TO CONTROL
B-27421 TIMOTHY LEARY, A-2983 MALCOLM X,
PANCHO VILLA, REPORT TO CONTROL YOU HAVE
VISITS!** your i.d. card matched with a
note/two barred gates/strip search/get
naked/rub your hair/open mouth/ears/
hands/armpits/lift balls/turn/open your
ass/keester stash/left foot/right foot/
ultimate degradation/more gates/plastic
room/match notes/visitor/visit/tension/
freakout/soledad institutional j.c.'s
will polaroid shoot you and your loved
ones for $1/eat money machines/mafiarun/
YARD UNLOCK! what's the scam/my celly
doing the big bitch/got drove on by some
jive assed motherfucking honkie/turned
out/buttfucking/snitch dropped a note on
him/dogfucking gooners locked him down/
the 6 month progam/appear before commitee/
**A 29498 ELDRIDGE CLEAVER REPORT TO THE
EAST GATE IMMEDIATELY!** radio that shit/
his crimepartner snitched off his batch
of pruno/go get your stuff/i'llmeet you
in the third tier shower/we'll get down/
6 packs for a good shank/zone the wingbull/
fuck all that shit!

YARD RECALL, ALL CULINARY WORKERS REPORT TO THE CULINARY! turn in your property/to r.&r./
sell your debts/two for three/to a collec-
tor/who's running a store/got apsych referral
rover boy approved you for vacaville/roll up
your shit/get some edison therapy/stressprogram

WILHELM REICH, REPORT TO THE ADULT AUTHORITY!
on the hot seat/annual hearing/15 min./ ta-
king them 3 clean/indeterminate sentence/
life top/you're now an institutional conve-
nience/don't bring us any more 115's/ we'll
let you know/one year denial/get an 18 month
date/dressouts/ruapp/work furlough/violation/

LAST CALL, ALL CULINARY WORKERS REPORT TO THE CULINARY! difference between steak and ham-
burger/hamburger made with sawdust/steak
comes from industries/seconds/filthy spoons/
blacks right/whites left/chicanos inbetween/

B-47450 BENJAMIN SPOCK REPORT TO YOUR WING COUNSELOR! board report/central file/128's/
policy of the adult authority/refix your term/
keep the place full/just before budget time/
grade 2 inmate/medium b custody/request for
interview/july board/101/h.v.p./orientation/

PREPARE TO RELEASE INDUSTRIES AND MAINTENAN-CE CREWS ONLY! do your own number/walk slow/
drink lots of water/lifer with a juice card/
send a kite with a freeman/front him off/

PREPARE TO RELEASE VOCATIONAL SCHOOL! THERE WILL BE NO PRINTSHOP THIS AFTERNOON! how
much time you got left/30 days and a wakeup/
selling the birdbath/for 10 boxes/streetclothes

PREPARE TO RELEASE ACADAMIC SCHOOL! teach a
duck/to make a fifi bag/get your ducats/he
just drove up/vasa cook on the streets/got
two 5 to lifes running wild/a 7 year board/

PREPARE TO RELEASE FOR THE YARD! stupid
motherfucker got some sniff/put his busi-
ness on the tier/i'll have to beef you/

ATTENTION! HUEY NEWTON A-11782 REPORT TO CON-TROL! administrative reasons/throwing a writ/
he got in the wind/over the fence/sallyport/

YARD UNLOCK! bone that hammer/driving a cad-
illac on the yard/i got those roses from
my running partner/you got any money on the
books/dont shine me on punk/sound on him/

SARGEANT TRUMP CALL 263! been here 18 years

mean motherfucker/inspection/shakedown/tier
loitering/tuck in your shirt/get a haircut/
YARD UNLOCK! get back to your house/eager
mail shoved under your door/nothing again/
some sancho fucking your broad on the bricks/
doing hard time/approved correspondent/
**ALL INMATES REPORT TO YOUR QUARTERS, START
COUNT START COUNT!** when you are first made
prisoner they tell you/our main job is to
count/3000000 prisoners in amerika/ counted
5 times per day/in facilities/big business
**THE COUNT IS CLEAR, RELEASE FOR EARLY CHOW
AND DIET LINE!** got a milkcard/7th lineup
of the day/busted for eating twice/step
slap beans/step slap potatoes/sten slap cab
bage/30 gal. black/coffee?/greasing/last call/
**ATTENTION, THE COMMUNITY AWARENESS GROUP HAS
BEEN CANCELLED, PREPARE TO RELEASE 6:15 UN-
LOCK!** point for me/i got some splivvy dope
towel exchange/here comes the bull/the shit
comes down/busted for cell visiting/fuck you
PREPARE TO RELEASE 6:30 CELL MOVE! third
tier for grade 3 only/stash your piece be-
hind the shitter/get off my case/you rug/
YARD RECALL! second draw canteen/270 smo-
kes in a can of bugler/street shoes/ a shot
of coffee for a tailormade/walk it off/
**ATTENTION, THE ALCOHOLICS ANONYMOUS MOVIE
WILL BE SHOWN IN THE PROTESTANT CHAPEL!**
playing tonk with a straight deck/for one
and two/the first four benches on the right
hand side of the tv room are for chicans/
last call clothing exchange/he locked up/
couldn't pay his debts/who'd he give up?/
**ALL INMATES REPORT TO YOUR QUARTERS, START
COUNT, START COUNT!** cell/5 by 9 by 7'6"/cot
steel cupboard/shitter/4 by 6 floorspace/
keep walls bare/on the shelf/you got a
writeup/hauled off to x wing/send it to
long beach/here i sit/in these blues/
another body/body receipt/countersigned/
doing time/satisfy the state/rehabilita-
tion/WHAT????/
THE COUNT IS CLEAR! THE COUNT IS CLEAR!

october 15 1970 *Sb*

A FANTASY NAMED MARY

all my life, i
clanged my gentle sword
against the fierce universe/
trying to slay the eternal past
and lay low the gallant future...

and so i arrived
in the cellblock country
studying time's tactics/
and with myself on my side,
blasted and iconoclasted
the invincible barriers down.

and so i found
the words which scorched
desire's burning heart
and the notes which stung
away the huge human distance...

then, over a heap of gods dead
and a pile of swords broken by
the breath of my all-night songs/
memory i murdered; ideals, i slew;
heaven i erased/ and hell i stomped
out, my fists and feet fierce agains
the gentle universe...

and so i lived to see
the past and future die/
          only to find that in the
          cellblock country there is
          No Now worth living in:

--now, the virgin, harped
and hollared

--now, the Virgin, harped
and hollared and demanded
that Truth in Love master
each moment's Purity of
Nowness; and without Love...well...

and so i had a bad bout
with the blues/ and after
conversing with my old friend,
Suicide, i stumbled across a
red-feathered fantasy/ and
with wings of rage and relief
flew back into the future like
a white crow celebrating the
madness of life, ringing
jingle bells in July, and making
salvation's little gesture by taking
bouquets of sacred dirt to
a fantasy named mary...

BANKS AND BOMBS

Blank blank blank
that's what's in my tank
maybe something rank
thinking about something
that really stank
like the stagnant garbage
in Big B's bank.

What is this?
Oh! those words again
written in this pig pig pen
again again and again
but never again
not even for ten
like eight nine the
big fat hen.

Even Uncle Ben's
CONVERTED rice
is too good for the mice.

Think twice
the whole world could be nice
but first
get rid of Uncle Ben
Uncle Toms
and best of all
Big B's fucked up bombs.

march 1970

NIGHT SOUNDS IN PRISON

In this beginning of another night
alonely,
I hear the heartbeat of my unborn son

And from the far dark bog
                    triple chin frog-princess
                                    croaking
golden eyed & glisten green
unseen

            A smothered cry,
            far off rattling of keys,
            twisting bedsprings,
t h e m i d n i g h t t r a i n c
                                  o
a gate clangs, locked   m
                                  e
to left and right, above below,s
                                  b
men breathing,   y
                    heavy stepping guard

august 1970 ♌

FROM HELL: "HAIKUS AND HOPES"

THERE ARE VIBRATIONS
YET WE'RE NOT AWARE
COUNTING TIME
WE HEAR NOT
SEE NOT
BUT
ALL IN ALL
THEY'RE THERE

FROM UNDERWORLD'S INFERNO
SHADOWS LOOM
SEARCHING GRAVEYARDS

SILENT WINGS GLIDE
ON WHISPERING WINDS

AUTOMATONS WE'LL BE
IN NEAR FUTURE
PLACED AND
REPLACED

TIME
THEME
DEATH
TIME REBORN TO TIME

**

GOLDEN SUNBEAMS
DANCE
FROM PEAK
TO PEAK

SILENTLY
WATCHING
IN EMPTY
WINDOWS
AS LIFE
PASSES
    LAUGHING.

A CHRISTMAS TREE ON THE LEVEE

Today you were here,
only a few thoughts ago,
but now your body has gone away
until our time comes again
in seven more suns
and Quan Yen will say we are the ones.

I see you right now
in the reflection of the sun,
riding in your red machine
with your sister
and the groovy head
in the dirty old blue jeans,
polluting the air
as it is almost everywhere.
Is that your long gold hair
or is it the sun's glare?
shining trough the window on mine,
so fair.

Cal Tjader is here
because I hear him very near.
Soul Sauce is the name of the ride,
it reminds me that I once died.
How many times have you cried
before I learned to glide
On this beattiful slide.

Tell Jose
it was real groovy today,
what more could I say
until they come another day.
I know what I feel
is all for real.

Stop!

Iron Butterfly,....heavy!
making my head go as fast as a chevvy.
Is that a Christmas tree,
I see growing on the levee?
Or is it something I see
in the future of my life?
with my children and
beautiful wife.
Yes! But until then I will
feel the pain of the deadly knife.

Stop!

Time for scarf,
sometimes I almost barf.

Here again
but not with a pen.
What then?
Clak clak clakity clak,
Clak clak clakity clak,
Then I push it back,
clakity clak,
down another track.
With you I want to crawl
in the sack
and devour you
like an exotic snack.

What was it that was black,
oh yes, a ball
hitting up on the wall
sometimes I almost had to crawl
or maybe even fall.
That rhyme makes me think
that it's you I need to ball,
but for now I'm locked up
behind these concrete and steel walls,
a building "they" call a hall,
a place full of menwho've all lost their
names, the day Big Brother
put them in chains
and with them he gave
a horn of plenty,
filled with nothing but pains,
even a number in exchange
for their names.
Why does man play such destructive
games?

I know they were wrong
but they think they are right
that $$ why it has been so long
that I've been away,
many a day
and many a night.
Is it with my life that I must pay?
Yet there are still more
that I must stay.

When we can play
games that are real,
I will show you all the love
that I feel,
it will be a place
away from the angry cold steel,
down by a stream,
with a rod and a reel.
Close to me you'll kneel
maybe even naked
after we peel.
Our bodies, beautiful and trim,
into the clear water we'll run,
yes That's it, for a swim
and after, make love
in the sun
with each other,
our life will be fun
hassles with our brothers
will be less than none
as we turn with a smile
to every one.

One makes four
and love makes more,
on the table, bed or even floor
makes no difference
if there is a door
because into your
beautiful body
a new life will pour
with a warm glow
like when you drink
a hot toddy.
Then we will know
how life must go.

march 1970

Vibrations.

Through time
continually evading vibrations,
coming through now.

Sounds in my head,
I know they are yours,
they feel like you.

Gently caressing vibrations,
swarming inward,
you are here, I know.

We have loved
erotically climaxed together
energy waves of our oneness.

My face is flushed
from the inferno
in your eye.
                *****

What can it be?

Feelings I cannot explain,
some are almost pain,
some really the same,
I think I am insane.

What can it be
inside of me
that makes me want
to see?

There is you, I know
but that is long to go
or was it long ago?

Oh!   now I know......
     ...too slow!

february 1968

THE MOUSE AND I

Where am I at? I can't find myself
everyone around me isn't moving;
they are watching me as I run

I found a talking mouse
he said I could come to his house
I knew I was there
because we sat and fixed cheese
I could never find this place twice
my head as ice

now the green stuff is flowing
down and up the walls

I just now came out of it
I knew where I was all the time
here, in my coffee cup.

MORATORIUM DAY

the tree grew pretty good where it stood
considering on pennsylvania avenue with
view -- its roots paved over -- mashed
and squashed by limousines and other
smog machines -- wedged in the crown --
side by thigh -- high -- out of range of
the teargas -- we had come to check up
on the state of the Union -- bewaring of
low flying stool pigeons we peered down
a green light tunnel and watched the
man -- nattily unsuitably suited -- sign
the multiple independent reentry target
vehicle appropriations bill into law--
politicaides huddled around the bic
click pen dispenser -- what else is
there to govern -- bargain from a
position of equal unilateral megadeath
and in the red corner a dilemma for use
to be caught on the horns of which.......

july 1970

PAPER DADDY

warrant paper
arrest paper
birth paper
legal paper
eagle paper
verdict paper
guilty paper
lie paper
sentence paper
rule paper
letter paper
photo paper
writ paper
shit paper
happy paper
sad paper
book paper
card paper
news paper
ducat paper
money paper
chrono paper

affirmation paper
denial paper
obituary paper
copy paper
fly paper and
more lie paper
transfer paper
body receipt paper
and more paper
but where is the
real paper
truth paper
reversal paper
pardon paper
discharge paper
even parole paper

hey mr man can i
exchange this
identity paper for
some zig zag paper
or some toilet paper

hey mr man can i
cut out a paper
man to send home
to be my kids
old man?

february   1970

2. Parole (Violator) Returnee - WRI and TPI arraignments per Review - personal appearance per Special Proceedings Cale

3. Review - personal appearance per Special Proceedings Cale or AA Resolution.

4. Special Proceedings - in absentia per Res. 216 (Receipt Miscellaneous.

5. P&CS calendar - per 3050 and 3063 P.C.

6. Executive, En Banc, Review, Special Meetings.

7. Executive Clemency Calendar (4812 P.C.)

SQUAW WOMAN

The one I love most of all
there she is
in the mirror
on your wall

red hair
green eyes
not small
big beautiful and tall.

Lips of honey
doesn't like money
winks kind of funny
like the Easter bunny
walks barefoot
when it's sunny

Bobby Goldsborough's "Honey"
Honey I'd love to be with you
if only I could
but Big Brother
doesn't think I should.
Wearing his pointed hood
Red, White and Blue.
He just ain't no good.

The one I love most of all
there she is
not in a mirror
just a picture
hanging
here in hell
on one of the walls
they call my cell.

may 1970

Baby, M_____ ____what can I say
to take the pres___ _____ day
the plac_____
with dishes ___
the baby cri____
no friend comes ___

your man still in prison and
the diapers stink and the sky

everything's grubby and the water is cold
all the clothes dirty; you're feeling old
as far as you can tell
today looks like hell
and tomorrow as well
you know of the faith yet it's hard to hold
that it would be this heavy you were never told.

on mornings like this there seems almost no hope
so much you've been forced to make do and to cope
you've had to be strong
already so long!
here's little to eat and you're flat out of dope
you feel you're about at the end of your rope
What else can go wrong?

I remember the fernhouse

the fence, built in

3 lazy days

the trips

up palo colorado canyon

to uncover

little wildflowers

and ferns

the dogs yard

with broken slats

I never fixed

digging postholes

for redwood and pine

and the landlady·

a lesbian of age

cypress shade with

the baby

tippytoeing on the grass

jan 1970

AGUA POTABLE DE MITLA
S.O.P.

"Agua es el mejor tesoro del mundo,"
child write exercise, brittle paper
under the sandal bare princess' foot.

Slow squeezed-eye around look
we stand in the square
                              glare
ovenhot   bake.

comes a maestro, stutter strutting on,
undertaker?

"Bienvenidos."

Powdergrey heat settles on his words
"Ah, si.....Canadienses
 I am the english teacher of Mitla."
 Wordperfect: "Welcome"
 Proud, next to the village well,
 Ching
 old dribble tap and tepid basin
 worn tule trees, birdshundreds.
 Vapid cabal.
We must immerse our heads
and hair
and hands
and do.
"No no amigos, es para tomar."
 What, that grey murk?
 Faux pas
 Blush heat retreat
 a cobbled spiral climb to the
 village rim
 past open door standing disapproving
 Zapotecas.
 Wasteful Gringos!

♌ january 1970

SHOW ME THY PHILOSOPHY

Show me thy philosophy   What hath
it created. A sling. That thou
mightest cast a stone of wisdom and
fell a thing that thou mightest lay
hands upon it?

Doth it stand upon its foundation in
an unalterable attitude, unmindful
of the winds of change, knowing not
the trickle of man's wit, stonily
staring forth, smugly
complacent in its knowledge.

Bring thy philosophy forth.

I shall wring it by the hand; I shall
know it. Doth it limp? I would then
lend it the hand of love. Is it blind?
I then would lead it. Isit in labour?
I then would look upon its begetting.

Aye, I would look upon the staff it
leaned upon, for if it be a true
philosophy, it shall lean upon but one
staff.

And that is the staff of LOVE.

1968 A

The Last Tree

Wandering through the planet's
　　　　last forest
Tree after tree withered & dead
Coming to a lone survivor
　Wilting and dying of thirst

　　　　Would you,
in dark gloom and sorrow
Reacting to endless dead waste
Give up, in empty futility
Or water that very last tree?

august 1970

FOR SALE

1 ROOM 6×10 COMBINATION KITCHEN TOILET BEDROOM DININGROOM GARAGE! WALL TO WALL CEMENT — STEEL BARS & BED

NO PETS NO KIDS NO WOMEN NO LOVE NO PRIVACY NO HEAT NO NOTHING...

LONG TERM FINANCING !!!

FRIENDLY KIND UNDERSTANDING LANDLORDS

Ecology Lesson #9

Have you heard   the word?
dig a hole   in the dirt
        make your turd
                fit
        cover it.

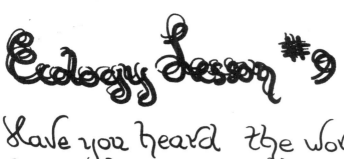

Wipe your ass with the leaves
of some plants
Watch the ants!
You'll learn the trick quick
don't try a stick
who wants crap in his pants
or on his hands.

Lets put fewer and fewer
feces in the sewer
Noone likes swimming
in shit
a bit.

                    SL august 1970

GRAPEVINE EAVESDROPPING

I lay on my bunk in my cell gazing into the black void. My mind races, listening to the echoing chatter, attempting to make-out the various dialogues that hum grapevine news and bullshit.

"How many did you get rid of?" "I'll be right back man, I forgot the catsup." "Bamm." "Whats wrong with you bitch?" Got alot of muscules back there, you can pull them all at once, you know?" "One of them big gorillas come in here." "Ya keep that seprate." One con stands on the second tier, he's leaning over the rail, brushing his teeth, scratching his ass, watching a pinochle game. "One deal, one deal, one deal." "Well I'll put one on ya." "I need a queen of hearts." "Thats kinda cheap." "No aces, jacks, or nines." "Forty in the pooper." "Fuck'en L.A.'s gotta win." "Six and twelve is thirty-six." "Whats happened to—" con walks up to another cons cell and sniffs deeply. "Hey man, whatcha rais'en? Hampsters? What do yeh got, a bear for a celly?" "Open that fuck'en windowman." At the end of a school trimester. "Still sucking ass?" "Thanks for the grade teacher." a con hidden from sight, beats viciously upon the metal schoolroom wall, teacher comments, "He must of received an 'F', most have received 'F's." "I'm taking roll goddamit." "You might be able to see this grade, aahh, no, to bad." con's comment. "Effort 'C', fuck him, grade 'C', fuck him agin." "Thats too much man, the cats in the class for two weeks, gets 'C's and I'm here for to months and get 'F's, wipe that shit off you're nose." "When your called to go ahead of the class, you just get on you're knees." Back at the wing, "I'll thrill your shit." "Your moher's shit." "I saw mommy butt banging Santa Clause." "What wing burned their Christmas Tree?" "Did you hear about the guy who received three jars of coffee in his Christmas package and because thats al he got, he smashed the three jars?" "Ya, I can see why he's here." "Six-four homie." "Hey homie, its all his fault." "Slap all the freckles ofa that punks ass." "Everyone needs a cold drink of water once in awhile." Inmates name is Applejack, "Hey Appleneck, yeh look better go'en than come'n." 'Call, call, pass high, pass out, raise." "Two boxes to yeh." "Whatcha do'en dufus." "I gotta ring my mule out." Crater faced, four eyed, tattoo of maryjane on his chest. "Ya good thing I'll be gett'en out some day, I'd hate to hafta turn out." "ALL INMATES TO THEIR QUARTERS, START COUNT, START COUNT." "Hey now this is the only joint in the fuck'en world with a pay phone in the main corridor." "What are you?, some sort of fruit fly." Inmate screaming from his cell, "Hey, Frank gimme a smoke." Frank uplifts arms as though to say I ain't got none, but his pocket buldges with a pack. "Fuck you then, you commie son of a bitch." A he-she across the way giving someone a show. Clad in panties, swaying his narrow ass from side to side. Wait, the mother whipped out his dong and now he's waving it flappingly, AT ME. I've been burnt. He turns out his lights, no chance for retaliation.

A barber talking about cutting hair in a convalesce home. "Yeh, where they can't fight back and ya gotta strap'en to the chair to hold them up, you could'nt cut a manikins hair you mother fucker." "Keep him off the streets." The lights are still out at miss things house, "Come on." Someone called. Yeh I think, 'Come on and flash a little rod, I don't care, it'll be a change in scenery, I said come on, your fuck'en up the fire baby, twisting the ego. Cat still screaming from his cell for a cigarette, "Assholes so tight their squeaking." "No, I don't lurk at my door." Cop walking along tier as though a flashlight has been misplaced. "Turn down that fuck'en recordplayer." I think I see two-way in the silhouettes of his cell. Guy still yelling for a smoke. "What are these?" he yells at the top of his lungs after a con gave him five tailor mades. "I don't want these fuck'en things, I ain't disgrac'en my lungs." "What do yeh think I am?, a fuck'en cigarette machine." Four cons sit on stools around a bolted to the floor table and discuss constryctive antics. "Hey, did you hear about that guy in F or E wing that stuffs things into his yang?" "NO!" they answer with great intrest. "Yeh, the cat draws a crowd and lets them watch him pack himself." Laughter, another con speaks, "What about that dude in North that buys dirty socks to chew the toes." "whaaat?" they exclaim with laughter. "Yah, the longer ya wear'em, the more he pays." "Whats that click, click shit?" "Some fool peck'en away on a typewriter." "Yeh, theres this guy in G wing the bull caught with a bag fulla dirty shots." Roars of laughter, "Yeh, your mother." more laughing.

Talking to a con that deals heavily in psychology he stated, "Yeh man, these cats around here are security starved. Look at 'em, the cells have been painted, concrete floors waxed, pictures and paintings hang from their walls, rugs on the floors, recordplayers, buying new comodes, shinning the bars and when they walk into another guys cell, their eyes rove over your property and silently scream GIMME, GIMME, GIMME, GIMME, GIMME, GIMME. Their all clinging and grabbing." "Ya," I said, "Gimme a shot of coffee, will ya."

My eyes are red and burning with fatigue, I sit on the shitter waiting for Miss Thing to do her thing, AAAH there she goes, why that jive bitch turned out the lights, No, there she is — WACKING OFF, Jesus, what more does a guy haveta go thru around this camp. Potbellied cops burping, farting, scratch ass, shittails hanging from pants, soup stains on ties, talking about up against the wall mother fucker.

Walking to the hospital's sick call line, you stop and your ear twitches, Asprin is the remedy. "Doc I've got a cold," "here take these asprin," sprained foot, asprin, tempature, asprin, diarrhea, asprin, head ache, asprin, shank in back, asprin, gun-shot, asprin, year denial at board, asprin, asprin, asprin. "Doc, doc, I'm allergic to asprin." Here, take these shitpills.

Sanitation is the cry at SOLEDAD, no smoking in school, chow hall, church, board room, gym, hospital. Its a sure way of stopping maggots in the bread, mice in the beans, ants runn'en in an out of cells, and cockroaches that scurry like wild fire thru your cell, climb the walls, and play kamikaze at your head eating the dandruff from your scalp.

When first arriving at SOLEDAD, I was thrown into the hole. That could of been mistaken for a public restroom. On the walls that have been painted uncountable times were carvings of busty bitches with stick legs, captions: fuck your mother cop, Black Panthers, K.K.K., George is a punk, droopy, snoopy, Viva la Revolution, jail is hell, suck my dick and Jesus Saves.

The inmate's most used word is FUCK, second most used is YOU, and the third is PIG. The third is gaining more stature. Pig this, pig that, pig, pig, pig, pig. The pig is the blame for any and all.

As I stepped in thru the East Gate with this morsel, a young correctional officer stated to another as he nodded my way. "Don't ask him, I know, their cocktail invitations for the party he's have'n tonight."

R.C.P.

KITING

I fly by night
on my radical kite
and see the machine
in all its gory.
Cities ablaze
New York, Las Vegas, Tokyo,
smog yellow haze,
horror show.

The forests are down,
our planet turns brown.
A horse or a hare
is exceedingly rare.
Lakes show white,
Huron, Erie, Ontario,
with bellies of fish
dying below.

Below the damns
rivers flow low,
life sacrifice
to demand for power,
carrying down,
Columbia, Snake, Colorado,
the trash of each town,
sluggish and slow.

Streams of offal
and d.d.t.
pour into
the sea.
Whales are few,
Pacific, Gulf of Mexico,
where many once blew,
none now blow.

Yet far from the prisons
and computerized greed,
with the strength of mountains
swells our new seed.

Inviolate junction,
Rainier, Everest, Kilimanjaro,
of essence and function,
radiant glow.
All L.A.'s have gone bust
with consumer lust...
Welcome age of Aquaruis,
age of sharing and trust.
Animals learn,
eagles, reindeer, buffalo,
they can return,
grow.
When I saw that sight
from my radical kite,
I came down in the dawn
among us, the people.
Black, brown, red, fair,
Zulu, Arab, Eskimo.
all our sons, all our daughters
and Aux.

march 1970

IN THE BEGINNING

In the beginning
she showed me her hair.
There
was dawn sun glow
and Sunday morning
city   all
around.
Let's face it, I was a mess
and looking for another chick.

                    said the lady:
"I'll go to the beach with you."

As we drive,
she shows me her eyes.
Yukon spruce? gold? green?
whatever.
Far altars of a
cool cathedral.

                    said the lady:
"Come closer, softly."

After a while
she shows me her
smile.
As a chinook,
bringing spring.
Buds burst,
birds sing.
I fit mine to it;
fits.

                    said the lady:
"Let's stop for coffee."

Then, on the sand
she shows me her
hands,
holding life, warm,
tender.
Go wave,
flow,
rise and let.
We got wet
in the spray.

                    Said the lady:
"Hey, I dig you, man."

Then in the evening
me and the moon
build a nest.
She builds a fire
and shows me her breasts,
curved, spaced
and equally
infinitely
nice.

FIRE!

                    Says the lady:
"I'm a woman,

NOW!"

april 1970

GLORIA

The glory of love

reflects in your eyes

as you feel me coming

far down the trail

I pause, let the butterfly

gather its nectar,

then I pick the white flower

for my love, for Glori.

The glory of love

sets your hair shining

as you hear my singing

from among the trees.

I kneel down to drink

and watch the trout jumping

bring a handful of water

for my love, for Glori.

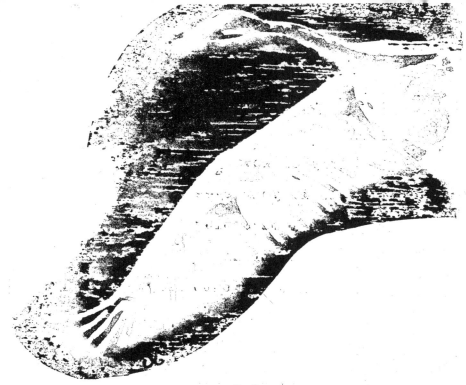

The glory of love
glows in your breasts
as you sense me running
through the spray on the beach.
my feet hurt like hell
on that damn sharp coral.
Let me pick up this pink shell
for my love, for ulori.

The glory of love
deepens your aura
as you see me skipping
down the hill, through the grass
In my pack is a feather
to stroke your cheeks with,
a gift from a falcon
for my love, for Glori.

The glory of love
blushes your belly
as you smell my chest,
arms tight around me.
I set my load down,
take our son on my shoulder,
while our lips taste the honey
of our love, our glory.

The glory of love
throbs in your yoni
as our life flows together
and we share in the wonder.
Then much later I'll tell you
of the long nights of waiting...

may 1970

"The Problems of Writing in Prison"

The problems of writing in prison you ask? Did you ever lie on a steel prison bunk and listen to the insanity that rages on the concrete tiers? The gasp of a dying man, stabbed brutally to death? Ever watch a man go insane? The embers of intelligence frozen with madness. Have you lived like a hermit in the nine by five cell furnished by the tax payers? Ever been in one of the prison holes? Darkness man, ever where, cold pavement, a hole in the floor to shit in. Crazed animals chained in the cells of terror, fed by the insanities of a sub-culture of humans. And you talk about the problems of writing in the prison system.

Have you abided by rules of oppression that stale mate the mind? Has your mind ever reeked with firey hatred, inflamed with the help of degeneracy structured by an indolent prison structure? And you ask about the problems of writing in prison.

A chance walk by the visiting room door brings the slight whiff of the woman smell, wild and musty. Ever been with out a woman for seven years? Have you tried to coat your feelings with sheets of steel to ward off the comments of stupid people? How many times have you had your back against a brick wall in the middle of a riot? A knife flashes at you from the crowd of savages. Nothing personal as the blade slips into your precious skin, you just happened to be there. Ever see your blood rush out like a giser? I've seen others.

Let's have a breakfast of peanutbutter and crackers, and a lunch of that also. It's too bad I missed the thirty second cell unlock to go to the chow hall. It doesn't matter anyway, nothing but grease and sour food there. What did you asked about the problems of writing, and the problems of writing in the prison system?

If you are an artist, have you ever been told what to paint? And what not to paint? And when you do sell, the fat cats of the prison system deducts twenty five percent. It's the same with a book or story. I see people coming that I can't avoid, to be rude to them would be cause for a killing, for they know nothing else. I chuckle in merriment at the writers of the free world who bemone their problems of writing.

I have looked at a yellow wall for seven years, it has become my wife and my children. Sometimes in the stillness of the night it speaks things to me I dare not tell. The things it has seen men do inside these prison cells.

Shock has ceased to register as I see two men locked in a lovers embrace. Where are the puritans of the free socitey? I want them to see their children.

I'm told I must be rehabilitated. This is the enviorment that is going to do it for me, they have told me so. The problems of writing in prison, there seems to be a few, doesn't there?

Pink and purple
came to visit
pink and purple
came to stay

in their basket
was some candy
and their toes
were made of clay

pink looked purple
after sunset
purple pinkly
in the day

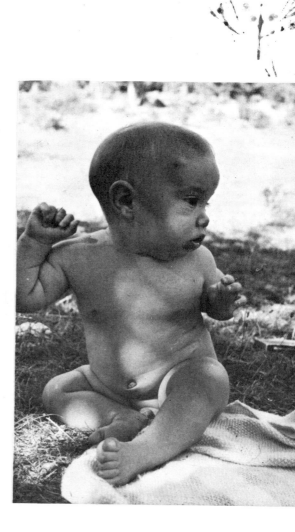

ALWAYS EASTER

I wear a purple egg
all over inside me.
So slow did it grow
that it's still quite new,
you helped it get born
without breaking.
Its function is to
do,
with the one in you,
what purple eggs
always,
everywhere,
do
together.

But it seems
to crack easily
and if you slowly break it,
I won't know
until

it's too late.

To fix it

or fake it

won't work.

Growing another

takes almost forever,

it's a hard job to match it,

you must constantly watch it

and can never get

quite

the same colour.

So grownouts, I beg

you,

don't squash

or mash

my purple egg

you

seed me

I need you

to feed me

then heed me

I'll lead you

to the space

where purple eggs

hatch.

In the warmth

of each other

out sprout

white ~~fairies~~ fairies

and elves

diapha nous

play

in radiant

rhythm

continuous

do

everywhere

together.

july 1970 ♌

SHALL WE PLAY

Come out tonite
the birds are down
and flowers closed

        just ahead you'll see
        the bridge, step on
        gingerly

run your hand
along the cables
of white moonlight

        skip along the deck
        of stretched clouds
        puffing fluff

look below, girders of
warm winds rise
up to carry you

    arching from green
    black forest pier
    to mountain crag and on

then just a whiff
,of fragrance from a
nearby star

    brings wonder of being
    so far, yet here is
    coming near

that's where I wait
for you tonite,
our tent is warm.

june 1970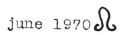

in the stu
lives an
when the
he flies o

but on nights that
he rides on our cat
with a saddle of re
that he hides in a vat

picking pansie
that he weaves in h
I just told you a s
what do you think o

np by the street

els with a hat

moon has a hole

n a bat

are windy

ves

and daisies

a mat

tory

& that!

SPRING MORNING... CINO

Sanu paws my cheek.

"Go away"

Shaking,

a glistening spray of dog...

cold on my chest.

"Come on then, lets explore."

Hush dog! A warbling thrush ?

Fair in the shadows of a redwood ring,

strong and silent giants,

crowns sweeping the sea blown sky.

You laid there, warm, still,

smiling.

Perhaps a dream of love just spent.

Around us a witch circle.

Freshorange toadstools,

just thrust through, needle clung.

With tiny orchids, fragile purple,

in your outstretched hand,

hair halo on the herba buena,

sunsplash on your belly.

I watched a while and didn't wake you.

april 1970 D

I'LL MEET YOU ON EARTH

My brother told her
to come see me.
She did.
Walked with the sun
into our meadows.
Purple girl
knows the whirl
of the planet.

The message she came with
I didn't catch.
When you see a flower
that walks,
you watch.
In her leather bag
with the broken latch
are the ching and tarot cards
also a battch
of tools and things
to cook food from scratch.
She can match your thing with
the planet.

She does yoga and stuff,

builds a fine fire.

Her hands are

quick with a needle,

tender with life

and strong with love,

as she lies by me

in desire

on the planet.

When the time came full

and her breasts shone white,

we made it together into

the white light.

The result of our flight

a wondrous child

just as she

  an Aquarius

and starlet

to the planet.

april 1970

THE MEADOWS VERSUS THE MAN

Freely we offered
but no.....

They came for our jewels
and our treasure.

We have but the green of the meadows,
red of the forests and our clay pipes,
blue of the springs and pink of girls'
cheeks.

Apples and berries and rice,
love and laughter and joy and puppies.

Out, out you all
The cheek, no grasshopper may live the w
winter through, the cheek.

february 1970 ♌

THIS

I came across one today two times
it was there in prayer by himself

The first time I saw this, it said:
"Have you seen my soul anywhere?"

The second time I saw this,
he found his body
and his soul
was behind his picture

As I sit now and think of this thing
I say:
"What could it have been?"

ORGONOMY 1970

the fond entrance into

        love's dancing eyes;
the shout of a rolling road,

        "Lo, I come away!"
the juice of fruit sucked,

        the splatter of pee;
a climb of spinning stars

        in love with falling;
trees singing to trees,

        birds brandishing swords
and today's sorrow slain,

        but not tomorrow's....

september 1970

Snowprincess

Snowprincess gathering

fiery sunset rays,

hands deft,

weaving a nest,

for nights of enchantment.

Now quick and quiet

'ere the stars claim their garden

and the moon is summoned

by the nightengale

onto its stately journey.

She folds with comely arms a

stretch of sky the colour of her eyes

and spreads a bed.

Her silken hair fragrantly

enfolds her breast.

With satin shadow smile she

thrums her drums, and hums and

sways in gentle strength and

warm and waits.

may 1970 SB

AFTER READING GINSBERG,
A LITTLE LOVE SONG

I HAVE FEELINGS THIS WILD NIGHT
WHICH ARE NOT TWISTED INTO NOTHING
BY THE EMPTY WINDS WHICH USUALLY
CROUCH BETWEEN CELLBLOCKS...

I HAVE A PARADE OF ELEPHANTS
STOMPING AROUND IN MY STOMACH,
THAT HIGH PRICED ORGAN WHICH
HAS NEVER FORGOTTEN HOW TO PLAY
TEN THOUSAND SONGS OR SO; AND TONITE,
I'M ALONE IN A SLOW JUNGLE
WITH A SCHOLARLY GUT, ALLEN GINSBERG,
YOU OLD LION.

I HAVE BEEN A'SCAMPERING AROUND
IN MY WARDROBE AND SORT OF GOING
THRU THINGS WITH MY LITTLE BLUE PAWS
TO SEE IF I COULD RUMMAGE UP ENOUGH
LEASHED PANDORA TO BEGIN A MOST
SCANDALOUS COURTSHIP OF HIS HIGHNESS,
BUT WITH TONS OF ATOMIC MUTANT EXPERTS
SLITHERING AROUND THE NEW BABYLONIAN
VEGETABLE, WHO CAN TELL IF
TWO POETSONS WILL MEET
AT THE JUNGLE SPRING
TO TRADE PANDORAS
AND HOMEMADE CLOTHES
AND RUB GUTS ?

1969

BLACK PRISON

MY BLACKNESS is almost gone
      i have sat here in prison
              and
lost all that thing called colour
      i have found the word no longer
               exists

yes
      it is strange
      i have gone beyond the colour
              line
      i see the rainbow
             but
      it has no colour at all
      it is all matter
MATTER the absolute nothing
      the all consuming everything
      i see words PEACE and LOVE
      i feel what it expresses
      i advocate what it dictates
      i have overcome the shadow
of death
      i am no longer alone in my
loneliness
      i have desired and found that
which i sought
PEACE   soon   LOVE
      the beauty is reality of fact
      which itself is fiction
a contradiction
      a belief in all that is
and is not
      i have found self and in finding
      i have seen my destiny
      i know where i am going and
how far i must travel
a few steps......even less
      if i decide not to go
i must go, it is calling
i must answer
i must heed its call
here i am   prison
      HERE I AM.

october 1970

Mother Love taketh

Her eyes were dark as with dread
Scorn, she considered me a child without
heart. "You I hate" she said, and turned
her back on me to walk through
the broken mirror of love forever lost.

I stood before the mirror for a long
time seeing no shape, form, or future
and the eternal pain of loneliness
stood waiting at the door...

People and Things

People saw with eyes like soap bubbles
Reflecting off the reflection's of the
T.V., the news, the glass,.
And finally off the reflections of
their own eyes

But still they could not see for the
blindness, of ones eyes, and ears, and
belif, and for ones primitive extractions
of origin.

Were they aware of their futile
horizonal zoom trojectory low
flying smells, the F.B.I. and long
Pall Malls, of polio infested
children in the halls?

of skys that are brown
of cigarette butts and the
dank musty odor of
coffee grounds
were they aware of
themselves?

deluech.

Once there was an old man
living by the sea
searching for flowers.
He lived all his life in a city
working in a factory
He could not find many flowers.

NIX-SON
STOOD STIFFLY PRESSED AGAINST
THE WALL   ARMS FOLDED
STARING   ...FLINCHED
WHEN THE BULLET SANG
FELL OUTWARD INTO
HIS STREET OF GOLD
ONE TOO MANY HOLES IN HIS HEAD
FOR BETRAYING AMERICANS

Strange cigarettes

Cigarettes from foreign lands
wrapped in funny paper
with different coloured bands.

You light up with fire
two drags, one more
hold it in, flying higher.

Enjoy your trip to foreign lands
listen to the music
making love and holding hands.

Now it's almost gone
only three more drags
you need a crutch.

The scent still lingers,
but it's gone
you've burned your fingers.

february 1968

HOW TO DEVELOP A MENTALLY UNHEALTHY INDIVIDUAL

Having been given the problem of developing a mentally ill individual, I must first establish who I am and what powers I possess. I am Omnipotent with absolute power over all of my subjects. I have an excellent set of doctrines and rules which I can call upon anytime to enforce upon my people — such as the U.S. Constitution including the Bill of Rights, the Bible and various other law books which I utilize whenever I feel the need. My predecessors and I, over the ages, have carefully made these rules and guidelines establishing exactly what we expect of a subject.

When I find an individual subject who does not like my doctrines, I begin to feel anxiety, conflict and paranoia. This I will not stand for . . . however, that is not my immediate problem. I know what is best and right for my people, and how my subjects should present themselves to conform and adjust to my concept of society. Let me tell you what I do to someone who doesn't obey my doctrine.

* THE OMNIPOTENT FABLE *

Once upon a time there was a young man named Citizen who for a long time followed my rules. One day he started to misbehave by using addictive drugs, falling in love with a prostitute and developing other insidious behavior patterns that culminated in his being an obviously bad subject and a danger to my society.

Putting my plan into effect, I sent my protectors to arrest Citizen and put him into one of my prisons. Once I had him in prison the first thing I did was strip Citizen of his identity: I told him that henceforth he would be known as Six. Naturally this disturbed him; however, I did not feel that this was enough, so I told him he would be in prison for at least one year and possibly the rest of his life — his release depending upon when I felt he was ready to conform to my rules again.

As soon as I had stripped Six of his identity and future, I told him that he should spend his time in confinement meditating upon his crime, regretting what he had done, and to formulate new and basic resolutions about the future. Also, I told him that my primary objective now was to rehabilitate him with a prison-learned trade.

There were, however, a few things I didn't tell Six, things which he would have to find out for himself. Besides, I really don't acknowledge their existence myself as it's more convenient not to. But I'll tell you.

Almost everything that happens to Six in prison will appear unreal. The urgency of time passing will be forgotten — Six will go through each day usually only half aware of where he is. The only time the mist of unreality will dissolve is when crucial happenings occur, such as parole hearings or visits. For my protectors, this half life is a good thing — for the more unconscious the prisoner is of his surroundings and the more he behaves like an automaton, the better prisoner he is, which means the less trouble he causes.

After I have Six induced into a dream-like state he will function on a lower physical and psychological level. In fact, he may return to a condition resembling infancy and not help but respond like an infant to the events of each day. I will deprive him of his freedom of movement, and all of those qualities associated with manhood. I will feed him, take care of his needs and tell him where to go and what to do. In essence, I will make him a child again.

At the same time, I will demand from him the behavior of an adult. If he doesn't respond I will break him by what is called discipline pounding him into submission — psychologically of course, and accustom him into being dependent. My protectors will be omnipresent to insure my demands are met. All round him will be an atmosphere of punishment and denial, degradation and rejection — the bars of his cell to the uniform of my protectors will scream out NO to him, causing his tensions to mount with each denial.

Then, for my rehabilitation program, I will place Six into one of many prison industry trades, telling him he will develop good work habits that will enable him to become a productive member of my society and capable of earning a good living. But I will not tell him his job is existent only to keep him occupied so he will not become a threat to my security, and to become the cause of trouble and unrest. I will not tell him much of his working equipment is old and badly outdated, that there are few exceptional teachers to help him, and the poor teachers far exceed the good ones. I shall probably keep him on one job, performing one minor detail of a project's operation, if only to keep him occupied.

Finally Six's mind will become a battleground of conflicting emotions; he will have to choose between a dream which will keep him sane and a reality which will drive him mad. This is the time when Six may blow his top and become physically or mentally ill, or even strike out against his environment and the people in it with blind rage and fury. He will feel frustrated, blocked in every goal that life has to provide, cut off from every normal desire and being helpless in the absolute sense of the word. He will be pushed around by the whims of others, and there will be nothing he can do about his circumstances.

And when I have accomplished all of this I will set him free, releasing him into a demanding world which will require he act as a mature adult. Will he survive? Well, he had better or else I will bring him back for more of my rehabilitative treatment.

F.G.L.

SECOND TRUMPET WHISPER
(excerpt from the lost train)

while Time grinds to smouldering death/
fleshfumes stink/ pain strangles/ and
flattery swings hippie bangles/; i'll
not batter you with pontious pilate
smiles/ or go wild on your doorstep
for a penny/ or stand in your trickline/
or sell solutions/ or peddle answers/
or play your favorite song/ or say i
belong to gong-beaters international
communist corps/ or run an ashram hash
house/ or refuse to kill a mouse or rat
slowly amputating my leg/ or beg for
sex-thrills/ or a chance on stage/ or
make advance amends for excrement-
freak attitude/ or apologize for Life's
foul manners/ or pretend that you
muse-people give me no reason to round
up flames to whip you with from mad
train traveling seven simultaneous
directions beneath frightening flow of
firecracker thoughts shooting forth from
fountain of embers in blazing torment--
each one i must ride like separate
trains diving through space in dying
anguish of impossible desire...through
billowing beauty of living clouds/
awful in their movings/ and striking
silences so loud, the sky and i
tremble, while earthquakes are born
from a hard rain of falling trains--
hailstones of too many seasons spent
in hell watching waterfalls of white
creamfire drenching horizons with cosmic
sexlove untouchable...while foolish
rockets cloud the view...starve the
starving...and Relief is seeing pale
crimson fire earthworms tangling bodies
on emerald leaves of Whitman-grass...
as Whitman himself acts like a wheel

with a bad itch millstoning an angry
coffin...and america is a snake
swallowing screaming mice while a
wino's heart explodes in the gutter...
murder, malice, and jealousy shake
hands in the suburbs...useless war
beats ear drums...science supports
insanity...justice feeds hypocrisy...
and fallen angels weep and think
about apologizing for a tiny blue
chorus of horrid achings choking up
the throat while vulgar muse with
acetylene torch love welds hurting
heart to the hub of things--there to
forever perish in cherishing the
life and flame of same old train.

LISTENING

I stood a long time listening

   and

      hearing the truth

          only

went searching for a lie

         and

   finding one

I stood a long time listening

        but

it was the truth

     and now I

   have trouble hearing

"The Magician"

The cell block was quiet now. Pausing for a moment, the guard flashed his light on my bed. Satisfied, he passed on to the next cell. Softly, a radio played in the darkness.

Closing my eyes, I let the thinking part of my mind drift into neutral. Instantly, power and energy flooded my body of flesh. Very gently the light in my body started to expand. Shafts of light seeped through the pores of my skin. Radiant hues of iridescent colors merged as the atoms of flesh gently broke up. A sudden blaze of White light, and the small prison bed was empty. Evenly the atoms had returned to their natural state.

I could create, become a bug, merge with a distant star, or flow as water in the distant mountain springs.

Swiftly I formed a body in the cell bed. I even breathed the spirit of life into it. Sitting up in the bed, it looked at me with a smirk. I let it look around for a moment or two, and put it to sleep.

Swift as a thought, I sped to the rim of the Universe. Distant Galaxies greeted me with vibrations of consciousness as I passed their boundaries. Constellations shimmered in the wake of vast quanities of exausted hydrogen. Brilliant stars burst into octavies of Divine melody as I passed by. Expanding my consciousness, I passed beyond the fringe of Creation. Beyond the limits of the created, I passed into the region of the unmanifested.

Great masses of energy swirled around me. Instantly they stabilized as I passed through them.

At a whim, I created a Galaxie. Then I let it disipate. New images danced around me. Millions and trillions of Souls yet to be born. Leaving this panorama of half dead and live creations, I sped onward.

Great bursts of light rippled before me. The abode of the Titian Gods. Magnificent Celestial Cities of Light, arrayed in splendor, floated far above me. Young Gods, creating their fanticies.

Billions and trillions of light years sped by. The Souls of the dead lay slumbering in particles of blue mist.

Deeper and deeper, I penetrated into the vastness. Zillions of light years ahead, I glimpsed the Father of the Universe. Blazing white light, streamering fragments of Him — self in all dirrections.

Great buffets of energy and power struck me. My consciousness soared onward. We were merging. I could feel it. Probing each other with fingers of light, we danced the Song of the Spheres. Humble love flowed between us. Lovers we were, acting as clowns in the Universe. He fed as I nourished. Gently, with delicate movements, He pulled me to the center of the Cosmic Breast.

A warning rippled through my light body. Something was wrong. Instantly I was back in the prison cell.

The body that I had given life to, sat on the bed smoking a cigarette. Slowly I started to dissipate. I was dissolving. It mocked me, this hideous thing I had created. It had stolen my mind.

G.H.

R.I.P.

WHEN MOLOCH
GODS DIE
THE MYTHS
ARE LIFTED
FROM OUR BACKS
. . . . PEACE BE
WITH THEM...
THEY WERE. . . .
HEAVY.

THE NECESSARY TYRANT
AND THE REVEALING MINUTES

my my, you minutes
struggle and struggle by,
like san fransisco spiders
on the way to miami.....
stick around; i've no one
to tell tales of hell to but
myself and you Minutes
rattling by as i chew up chains
and stroke insomnia's dreams/
....and you chew up the faded
leftovers of my yesterday phantoms
....and you chew up the impossible
flesh of the mother of rainbows-
NO, you Minutes had better go
and be quick about going/
before i bomb Big Ben
with my atomic pen
and point out to men
that the mother-father
of Minutes is TIME, and TIME is
the most holy and
greatest benefactor
of MANKIND; and
TIME also commits
the most holy and
greatest CRIMES; and
TIME and CRIME are
both IDEAS born
of MANKIND-   SO,
JUST LISTEN TO THIS YOU MANKINDS:
you got me locked up here for
our ideas
and i think it's about time
you shared the burden
of all this thinking and
either let me loose
or remove the
threat of

                "yard recall!!!.."

october 1970

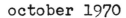

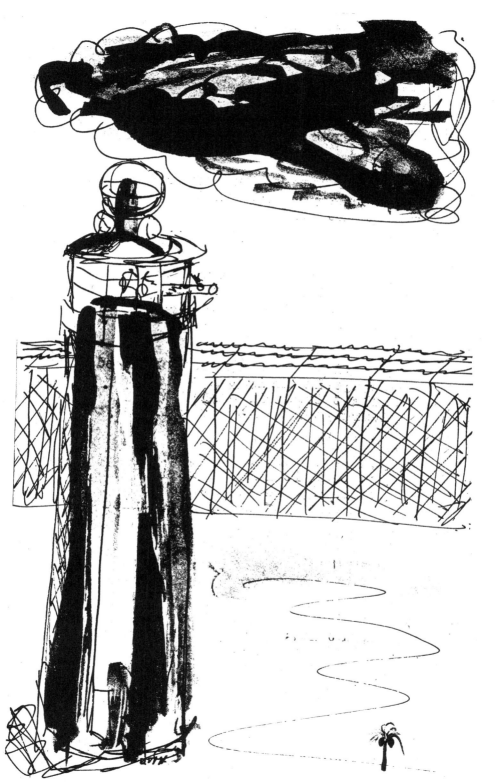

A SUNNY SOLEDAD AFTERNOON

so the day turned to lead
and the night to pig iron.
we found ourselves lacking
tickets to the new Earth/
lacking frontiers to pioneer/
and lacking the necessary
meshing gears to continue
the planet-wide mistakes.

our mechanisms bamboozled
by rebellious life energies,
the political hooligans and
the mechanics of civilization
sent us to the repair shop,
and here we sit/ drummed and
deafened by time's awful noise/
and assualted by technicians:

    (chorus of loud speakers:
    "PREPARE TO RELEASE FOR CHOW!!!"

we are being fixed.

and here we sit/ the disobedient
flowers in the hair of the rising
apocalypse giant--i sing in his
ear and he is furious and beats
me with keys and metal anti-music:

    (chorus of loud speakers:
    "S-SQUAD, REPORT TO THE VISITING
    ROOM! IMMEDIATELY!!!"

we have seen the gestapo before.

and here we sit/ our criminal
cocks being felt or nearly missed
in countless shakedowns--they do
not even know what it is all about

when they peek up our
bare asses looking for
stashes?

(chorus of loud speakers:
"REVEILLE!!! REVEILLE!!!"

THEY ACCUSE US OF SLEEPING TOO LONG.

and here we sit/ listening to
tax-dollar trumpet notes grind
against the blue and starry rotunda
of the voting sky/ crying like clouds
trapped in caves:

(chorus of loud speakers:
"MR. MORDOR'S GROUP COUNSELING
CLASS WILL MEET TONIGHT IN THE
CHAPEL!!!"

the paychecks laugh in the
supermarkets, banks, and billfolds.

(chorus of convicts:

come then, citizens, into the
penal pits and claim us. come
claim the tortured sons suffering
toilet paper destiny. come and
share our rue soup, zoological
violences, and our common goals
to nowhere but gone. come watch
how state-devoured identity makes
mighty men meek and meek men
murderous. come consider how he
who once lacked something, lacks
everything now. come see skeletons
tripping off the ends of monotone
tongues and come hear the clatter
of bones shattering on fragile
stone floors. come view the solid
wall horizon echoing empty-eyed

stares until despair drinks dry
the will to look. come touch the
polar flesh and halt the sexual
misery and wash the icy white feet
which pace and pace and pace toward
an unspoken hope that perhaps someday,
someway, you will no longer need
human trojans to protect you from
impregnating yourselves with your
own rotten sins rolling down the
devil's road like vicious glaciers
gobbling up the warm and innocent
pedestrians who came to the Earth
to live, and in living, walk ways
unwalked. come then you cowards,
and spare us not one dream of other
life in other places in other times;
spare us from your dangling prizes
for successfully tangling the wailing
strings of our rebel spirits into
knots so we too shall never sing
one original song nor breathe one
innocent breath. spare us from your
conniving charity and investments
against the certain doom of your
systems and mechanics and machines
which exalt cowardice and hate to
incredible fascist thrones which must
of needs tremble and shout and
condemn with pitifully empty words
the fullness of the convict poets
singing for one hour on a sunny
soledad afternoon...

and thus, we go
unnamed to protect
our fullness from
massacre

DID THE LIGHT REALLY
COME FROM HEAVEN?

ON LEAVING LIMBO

...to the leaving Sun,
our promise is cast...

come, soulless angel/
my antique child friend;
our lost train leaves
Limbo bearing nothing less
than alphas, omegas, and
aimless flesh on fire;
nothing less than the
solemn jangle of jokers
looking for a fresh laugh;
and nothing less than
robes of woven moonbeams
concealing our wounds--
    the tattoos of fate/
and hiding our huge pain--
    the false crown of destiny.

O Sun! we'll come stealing
children/ tying them up with
poems/ and spanking them with
music and joy productions.

O Sun! we'll come fathering
resistance/ holding pennies
up against the raw dawn/ and
with our patched guitars
playing magic songs.

O Sun! we'll come dancing
in abandon around bonfires
like devoted savages/ the
one drum behind all heartbeats
thumping loudly; we'll come
dancing because the undancing
do murder; one day they do murder--

O Yes! they do they do they do!
...one day, after they cannot
deeply fuck and deeply dance,
they do murder and stand aloof
from dancing. i hate you kinds
of citizens, i do i do i do!

...THE TRUTH IS HERE NOW,
   SO LISTEN TO THIS:

we are proof, (and not aloof),
that the Great Machine's War
against Life is lost. it is
defeating itself by creating
music and abandoned dancers.

HAS A SINGER EVER BEEN SHOT
WHILE SINGING?

HAS A DANCER EVER BEEN
ASSASSINATED WHILE DANCING?

...so, we are leaving now
to load our lost train with
more songs, more poems, and
more bonfires.

our sojourn in Limbo
is nearly over; we've
stood studying heaven
and hell on Earth from
our third-tier soledad
windows and shall soon
leave here loudly singing
the quiet now. we shall come
back to the Earth refusing to
cooperate with other exalters
of Limbo who shall in vain ask
us to lay today's footprints
in tomorrow's snow...

THE TAROT ORACLE

the **Fool** is caught in a
rain of philosophy, but
descends thru the Generator,
the **Empress Venus** and the
Emperor Aries Intellecto,
who are married to the
Cosmic Conciousness Boys
of the Earthbound Spirit
School, the WORLD, Number
Twenty-One.

In the WORLD, surrender to
a higher Being, the **Hanged Man**,
and bowing to the magician
goes on and takes place--
because the **High Priestess**
desires to accompany the
Cosmic Conciousness Boys
until the waves of the book
splash sperm on her blood-
stained ankles and the clouds
are talking and the book
starts a parade... another
happy ending darlin', and
I need another place to go....

the voice of the universe

0 FOOL

III Empress   Emperor IV

WORLD XXI

XII Hanged
Man   Magician I

HIGH PRIESTESS II

BIBLIOGRAPHY

The Complete Works of:
Wilhelm Reich
Charles Baudelaire
Krishnamurti
Marshall McLuhan
Arthur Rimbaud
John Lee Hooker
Albert Camus
plus All Poets &
Artists & Bob Dylan
& Antonin Artaud

TOLKIEN & BLAKE & JOHN
BARTH'S: GILES GOAT BOY
KORZYBSKI
BENJAMIN SPOCK
ALICE IN WONDERLAND
THE POT OF GOLD (James Stephens)
THE CAT'S CRADLE
VOYAGE TO ACTURUS (Lindsay)
THE DIVINE ANIMAL (Westcott)
THE I CHING
TAO TE CHING

HERMANN HESSE
All good indian lore but NO
philosophy and definitely "NO" psychology!
IF you have lots of time read
DUNE (F. Herbert), PAUL GOODMAN,
HERBERT MARCUSE, NORMAN O'BROWN
B. TRAVEN

FAILURE OF POWER

The lights just went out, guess I need a new bulb, but I will have to wait until the morning to get one. Wait a minute, the lights are out in the hall and outside too, except for the special lights on the fence. I will just have to finish this in the dark, at least until the lights come back on......

This must be about the fifth time the lights have gone out in the last four years that I've spent behind bars. This time I really get a funny feeling about the lights; can't quite dig what it is though, like maybe there's more to it than just the lights going out. Well, looks like I'm just going to have to finish this in the dark......

About two hours have gone by now and they still haven't fixed the lights.

Sure don't feel tired, maybe I'll just stay up all night; The other prisoners must have the same feeling, because they're not taking advantage of this opportunity like they usually do. This feeling is stronger than ever now, but I still can't dig exactly what it is. Maybe it's just my imagination tripping out, hoping for something to break this monotonous routine; hoping for much more than that.....

It's morning now and they still haven't got the lights fixed yet. No bell to wake us or pig horn to scream at us. I guess they will open the doors in a few more minutes so we can go to our morning feeding.....

Another hour has passed and still they haven't let us out, my ears can sure tell too. The walls vibrate with all the screaming. Sounds worse than

a zoo at feeding time. What am I saying? This is a zoo, and we're all caged animals, no? Hey, what's the pig shoving under my door? Looks like k-rations! It is. Must be what they're going to feed us. "Say, what's happening?" "Say, man; Hey, don't shine me on!" "Hey, you motherfucking pig!"
Now I know something is happening, that pig sure looked scared, more than usual that is. Sounds like I got some thing started; everyone is screaming at the pig now. I sure wish I knew what was happening; but I guess we will have to wait for that like everything else. In the meantime I will do something to keep myself occupied......

I wonder if they will pass the mail out tonight. I'll find out pretty soon since it's about that time. Here comes the pig now, looks like he has some mail. Yea, he's slipping something under my door. What's this:

NOTICE TO ALL INMATES

THERE HAS BEEN A MAJOR POWER FAILURE AT THE MAIN POWER PLANT. EVERYTHING IS BEING DONE TO EFFECT REPAIRS AS SOON AS POSSIBLE. EVERYONE WILL REMAIN IN THE CELLS UNTIL THE POWER IS RESTORED. YOUR COOPERATION IS EXPECTED

THE WARDEN.

Who do they think they're kidding! I'm not buying that shit. Part of it sounds like it may be true, but "slightly" out of context. "Major power failure" I was afraid this would happen before I got out of here. Now there's no telling what will happen to any of us. The pigs won't let us go now, that's for certain. We'll just have to go for what we know, got to get out of this cell first though . . . . .

I wonder what my neighbor thinks about all this. Haven't heard a sound out of him. "Hey Jimmy, did you get that notice?" "Fuck them pigs! That's a trick and I aint going for it. There's a power failure all right but not the kind they say; they could fix that easy enough, but they're not going to fix this power failure, because all their power is dead, like they are. Hey, we got to get out of here or we'll rot in these cells, if they don't kill all of us you know. Think they will let us out of these cells?" "I sure do hope so, know what I mean, man?" I hear you brother, loud and clear; like you say, we got to get out before they kill all of us. I got to go find my old lady and kids before things get too fucked up out there. We got a meeting place so I can find her. Told her where to go if the shit came down before I got out and I would come there and get her; told her not to tell any one where it is though. Dig"? Listen man, I'll rap to you later, I got some heavy thinking to do right now. Like on how to get out of here. Maybe between the two of us we can come up with something. If they let us out to the yard we can all get together and do something about it. "Well, Later man, let me know if you come up with anything...."

I wasn't quite sure at first but Jimmy is thinking the same thing so it must be true. I'll go crazy if I don't get out of here now. Maybe I can volunteer to help the pigs pass out the k-rations, anything to get out of this cell. I will at least have a chance at getting out of here . . . . .

. . . . A week has gone by now and they still have us locked in our cells. No news, no mail and no visit today, Well, they wouldn't let me have a visit now even if she did come. If something doesn't give soon I think I really will go crazy. . . . . .

Well, it's just about dark

again, no lights, not even the special ones on the fence. They quit working a couple of nights ago. I guess a lot of the pigs have been splitting or something; cause there aren't very many around here anymore......

"Hey, what's that? Looks like some kind of soldiers!" "Hey, Jimmy, look over in the field by the trees! Do you see all them people!" "They look like a bunch of Che's Guerrillas!"

Yea, they're setting up mortars or something like that. I sure hope they're on our side! Maybe they're gonna blow the pig out of his ivory tower and get us out of there!"

Boom! Boom! bang! ....
"Wake up in there, Wake up, you're getting a beef for being late to work!"

... not the end..

july 1970

Revolution; a word designating the
      process of ongoing change in
      an apparent recurring pattern.

I; a word implying separateness and
      or designating an organism
      theorethically functionable
      in indivisible isolation.
      also known as the basic unit
      of social statistics and cap-
      able of suffering progress in
      technocratic gulps. 2) a time-
      ly, unique manifestation of th
      the cosmic energy, inherently
      capable of intuitive flow,with
      joy, unitybound.......

Institution; when any institution
      becomes more than the timely
      structured cooperative for
      equal specific benefit of all
      the participants,democratica-
      lly directed and non-trans-
      ferable, it <u>must</u> be strangled
      through forthwith withdrawal
      of our enegy,"cause it's the
      big killer of life-energy.

Money; a word describing the second
      most "evil" institution. If
      "they" try and give you any,
      whether named wages or welfar
      refuse,
Language; a word describing words
      the first most "evil" insti-
      tution. Emergency use only!!
Intuitive Matriarchy; the flow-
      strategy of conceiving, bir-
      thing,suckling and tending
      expanded and applied as
      social guidance.
Phougher;(pron.: huffer) joyous
Kudi; sizeable   hiding.
              antiorgone.

Habblecheck stands out on
   the soledad prison yard
      each time we get
        a day off
          from
      the printshop
and blows a tenor saxophone
   to the mountains.

i would like to think that
   the mountains,
      the trees,
      & the sun
                  are listening.

i recognize my imagination
   listening in them; but,
      the birds!   i know
      they are listening,
      but i do not know
      what they hear...

            different
            ears
            hear
            different
            sounds...

            bird ears
            hear a
            different
            Habblecheck.

KISS MY ELBOW

It Calms
Chalk squeek, Raw shriek
Rife , Life
Tension , Twisted
Below listed
Wide Screen - American Dream
New Improved
Stereo, Living Color
Con Micro Enzyme Political Inaction tambien
INSTANT OBLIVION
The imprint of her kiss
Still on my arm
At the Elbow!

ARE YOU WITH US YET,
LAWRENCE FERLINGHETTI?

in and out of the reality holes;
day after day/ month after month/
year after year--To wind up grubby
prospectors staking out claims on
the commas and comas of conciousness/
and whispering drunkenly to our one
muse: the Invisible Mule.

ARE YOU WITH US YET,
LAWRENCE FERLINGHETTI?

our leased dreams/
        converted into ice-fishing
        shantys by the landlord...

our sparkely hopes/
        scrubbed by busy young mothers
        and hung out in the rain...

our radical beauty/
        kidnapped by bottle makers
        from the vending machine factory...

our noble wit/
        drafted to carve initials in
        veitcong fleshtrunks...

our milky youth/
        counting gray hairs and guitar
        strings in the penitentary...

our christ-like intellects/
        stomping around the campus in
        circles dodging buffalo guns...

our communal experiments/
        sanitized out of existence by
        prophylactic paranoids sporting
        rent-a-hurtz flamethrowers...

our peace parties/
    investigated and deemed
    subversive and scandalizing by
    the C.M.B.I.A.M.R.D. AND THE
    D.M.P.A.I.C.U.2...

our magic music/
    declaimed by the whores of
    Politicky Fair as being
    unnatural infiltrators...

our rock festivals/
    sentenced to death by local
    henchmen defending their holy
    beltbuckles with anti-aircrafts...

our restless shoes/
    nailed to one place by civil
    service carpenters and destiny
    squashing passport denyers...

our poor children/
    twisted at the same schools of
    the same---damn! damn!
    and goddamn!!

     HĀ-RŌ RŌ-TEN RARRRRRRRRRR!!!

...but, our beginning shall remain
endless; and we shall yet reap our
spirit sowing; and we shall yet re-
invent our lives/ until they are
  found yet unfinished...

            THEN,
not alone will we wake with fort
hearts to paint blue spots green
and green spots sweet/ and sweet
spots to sleep...ah!, that's the
way it goes in this maddening
poem of life/ he one day does
sleep. AND ARE YOU WITH US
YET, LAWRENCE FERLINGHETTI

SEPTEMBER 1970

BREAKTHROUGH, RESOLUTENESS.

Symbolizes a breakthrough af
ter a long accumulation of tension.
Refers to a time when inferior people
begin to disappear.

JUDGMENT: One must resolutely make the
matter known at the court of the king.
It must be announced truthfully.
It does not further to resort to arms.
It is necessary to notify one's own city
The rules for success:
Resolution must be based on a union of
strength and friendliness.
A compromise with evil is not pos-
sible; evil must be openly discre-
dited, as must be one's own passion
and shortcomings.
The struggle must not be carried on
with force.

IMAGE: The lake has risen up to heav.
heaven. The image of breakthrough.
        Thus the superior man disperses
riches downward and refrains from
resting on his virtue, distribute
while you accumulate to avoid
collapse.
9 in the third: to be power-
ful in the cheekbones brings
misfortune.
9 in the fourth: beware of
stubborn restlessness.
9 in the fifth: RIGHT ON !!!

Change to: TREADING, CONDUCT.
           Success!

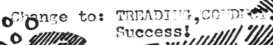

appendix

PREFACE:

When I first saw many of the poems in this book they were part of a small, hand-made book called **The 6:15 Unlock: A Kite from Soledad.** It was a very special book for me because, I can honestly say, it changed my life. How? Well, even though I've read **Soul on Ice** and **Soledad Brother,** even though I've thought of myself as a person with less than average prejudice, I realized as I looked through that book how much I had been prejudiced against men who have been put behind bars. Instead of the angry, hate-the-pigs, kill-the-honky voices I had been conditioned to expect from prison writers I was hearing men talk of flowers, of children, of the joy of sleeping with a woman you love, as well as the poems about the injustices of prisons — which I now saw much clearer than ever before. Men locked up for our crimes. Men able to laugh and cry just like you and me. I was teaching a Freshman English class the day I received the book; we had been reading a section of **Soul on Ice.** And I did what every English teacher does sooner or later, I asked my class how they really felt about Cleaver, about a man who was a criminal, a confessed criminal. And there were some who said, honestly, that they found it hard if not impossible to sympathize with a man in prison. Then I began to read some of the poems from **The 6:15 Unlock** and I passed the book, with hand colored drawings, with bits of flowers and pigeon feathers pasted to the pages, around the room. For the first time that day some of those students began to realize that their perceptions of men in prison had been as incorrect in their way as my ideas had been in mine. Both of us had made the mistake of underestimating the greatness of the human soul.

The 6:15 Unlock was dedicated, in a way, to a woman named Maria. A copy of her letter, written to Soledad to "Whom It may Concern" asked why the things her husband had made for her in the prison workshop and sent out to her had never come, even though his letters mentioned them. Across that letter was folded a piece of paper with these words written on it "Dear Maria, May It Concern Us." And this is the only dedication I can see to be made of this. May It Concern Us. May It Concern Us All.

Joseph Bruchac

The House of the Dead

Dostoevski wrote a book of his prison experiences and titled it **The House of the Dead.** The title is still appropriate even though the Russian novelist was writing about conditions a century ago and in another culture. The physical environment of prison has changed perhaps for the better since then, from the dark, damp, stony dungeon to the electrically lit, waxed and buffed concrete cell with its own sink and flush toilet. At least this is the situation on the main line in most of the California prisons. But this is all a smokescreen. The governor and the penologists want the public to believe that the prisoners are comfortable. So they constructed this **modern college campus,** as Time called it in a recent article about prisons. They also sent up a smokescreen of words. Soledad is not a prison. It is a **correctional training facility.** Guards are **correctional officers.** The men are not prisoners, they are **inmates.** They are not imprisoned, they are undergoing **rehabilitation.**

Bullshit, baby. (Guards are known as bulls or pigs by the prisoners). Bull shit. The truth is somewhere else. The truth is in these prisoners' writings. Read the list of prisoner slang words. Read "How to Develop a Mentally Unhealthy Individual." Read "Grapevine Eavesdropping." Read the book Soledad Brother: The Prison Letters of George Jackson. The truth is behind the smokescreen. The jailer with the whip and knout is still there but he has modern psychological weapons. Prison is still the house of the dead. Every day someone dies spiritually.

It is difficult to write a nice, neat, rational introduction to these writings. When I try to focus on what is happening to the men in Soledad I begin to oscillate with rage. And my rage is a luxury — because I have the freedom to come and go. What happens to a man who has to live with his anger in the daily frustration of prison life? He isn't allowed to express his anger. If he does, he will stay in prison that much longer. That is one of the games, the double binds they work on you. Anger has no where to go except inward and there it becomes depression and despair. Often the pressure of rage becomes too great, and a man knifes or kills a guard or another prisoner just to prove he is **alive.**

There are a number of evils in the California prison system. One of the major ones is the indeterminate sentence. A man is never sentenced for a specific period of time. It is two to twenty or five to life or some variation on this. When a man gets paroled depends on his behavior inside the joint, on how he plays the game. And from the beginning the game is negative and to his disadvantage. Everything in prison is structured on a negative basis. A man's file, his jacket, which is usually the basis for his parole, contains mostly negative information, infractions of the rules. Your persona is a negative one the moment you set foot in prison.

I am amazed that any writing comes out of prison beside letters, which is the true prison art form. The creative juice is sucked dry. Concentration is very difficult. Read the two essays on creative writing in prison. They tell it better than I can. As another of my students said one night as we were discussing the creative process, "In prison, you just keep bringing up the same old memories until you get sick of yourself."

I have said enough, although you can never say enough, about prison. I have only lived on the periphery of their daily suffering. Let the men now speak for themselves.

Bill Witherup

POST SCRIPT: These writings were smuggled out. They are anonymous to protect the prisoners themselves.

Joint Jargon

joint: a state prison

bull: prison guard

the man: same as above

the pig: same as above

beef: a reprimand given to a prisoner for an infraction of the rules. There are two types, 128s and 115s. The 128s are not serious, in as much as the parole board does not see them. But the 115s are. They are issued for such *serious* offences as eating twice, gar mouthing a bull, refusing to do what a bull orders, smuggling food out of the chow hall, possession of contraband such as hot dog books, sweat belts or a stinger. A 115 can be in many cases as good as giving a prisoner another year in the joint.

beef: can also mean the crime you are being held for

hot dog: a book or magazine that is sexually stimulating

hank book: same as above

stinger: a device made to heat water. Usually made of a wire with bare ends connected to two pieces of metal which is placed in water and shorts out, creating heat

committee: where a prisoner is taken when he receives a 115. This is known as a disciplinary committee and it is here that a group of guards and counselors decide what to do to you for transgressing prison rules. They can send you to the hole, give you work duty, etc. In this kangaroo court, a prisoner is not represented by a lawyer

hole: a section of the prison designated for hard core convicts. The jail within a jail. Commonly known as solitary confinement. According to law a prisoner can be held in the hole only twenty nine days. The prison system gets around this by designating part of this wing as the Adjustment Center. Men may spend years here, as did George Jackson

goon squad: a small group of guards that roam the joint looking for any infraction of the rules. They often search and mess up and rip off a man's cell.

shake down: when the guards search a prisoner, patting hands over the prisoner's body.

skin shake: entire search of the naked body. Poking and plumbing and combing of every hair and orifice

fish: a new prisoner

punk: usually refers to a homosexual

canteen punk: a prisoner that participates in homosexual acts for canteen goodies such as cigarettes, candy, coffee, etc.

joint turn-out: refers to a prisoner that has been forced to participate in homosexual acts

low rider: a prisoner that is loud and obnoxious. Usually can be found on the iron pile at sometime during the day, is often fighting or acting the hard guy.

iron pile: a portion of the yard set aside for weight lifting

gunsel: refers to a prisoner that is young and loud, always horseplaying, etc.

home boy: a prisoner from your home town. Usually shortened to "home." Such as "Hey, home, what's happening?"

celly: a prisoner assigned to the same cell. Also called "bunky"

snake: a prisoner that is known as untrustworthy and that may mess over anyone who becomes too friendly

rabbit: a prisoner who has tried or continues to try to escape

rat: an informer

to creep: when one prisoner ambushes another. Usually done to insure the victim will be taken to the hospital or the morgue.

burned out: when a prisoner has his cell set on fire. A common way of dealing with rats. Usually considered a warning by the guards, and the prisoner is removed to another cell block

burned out: also means to be completely bored with what it happening or not happening. You have the chow rotation memorized, the flicks, the surrounding scenery, etc. You are burned out, bored.

ticket: has many definitions, but usually means a contract for murder or a beating. In use, "He bought his ticket from Q," meaning a prisoner has been stabbed

contract: when one prisoner, or even a guard, pays another prisoner or a group of prisoners to murder another prisoner

a date: a parole date

dusted: murdered

kid: the term for homosexual that is owned by another

jocker: the "manly" or male counterpart of a sissy (punk). Usually considered to be a regular and not a homosexual, although he participates in homosexual acts.

regular: a prisoner that does his own number, does not rap to the man, and conducts himself as a man

wheeling and dealing: dealing dope or contraband or just about anything a profit can be made from. A wheeler dealer

shank: a home made knife

pruno: home made wine. Usually made of catsup, tomato paste, fresh fruit. Sells for five packs of cigs a coffee jar

piece: a shank, or a pipe or a club of some kind

kite: a short letter, usually smuggled out

sniff: any liquid that can be smuggled in and that when inhaled will get you high, such as carbon tet, rubber cement, etc.

prune: a man's ass hole

pad: the cell

house: same as above

box: a carton of cigarettes

box: a record player

grey goose: department of corrections bus for transporting prisoners

bonaroos: prison clothes that are starched or pressed, or anything sharp clothing

flashing: a visiting broad that flashes hips or panties or thighs

bogus: no good

snitch: informer

slammer: same as the hole

zone: to daydream. He's zoned out. He's on the zone

twilight: same as above

grease: to eat

streets: the outside, the free world

bricks: same as above

take his wind: take his life

take me on a trip: tell me about something, anything

let's jam: let's go

a hit: meaning someone got hit, stabbed

the bitch: a fifteen years to life sentence

nickel: five years

dime: ten years

nickel: five dollars

dime: ten dollars

jolt: the amount of time you serve. Like this is my first or second jolt

duck: a naive prisoner that lets himself be fooled into doing something

lame: a new prisoner unused to prison life

kick back: means to relax, kick back in your cell

hold your mud: means to perservere

tough it out: same as above

get the point: keep an eye out for the guard

stand point: same as above

bogard: to physically drive over someone

pull slack: to back up a friend

outfit: a homemade syringe made from an eyedropper and needle and spoon

fix: to inject into your vein

taste: a little bit. Let me have a taste of that stuff

stuff: heroin

smack: same as above

knockout: go to sleep

crime partner: co defendent

these are just a few of the slang words

INMATE MANUSCRIPT REVIEW FORM

Inmate Name:_Doe, John_ 'A' Number:_A-11111_ Date:_11/18/70_

Manuscript Type: Title
                                    ___Burgler Experience_____

Short Story   _____   Disapproved for following reasons:
Novel   _____ _____   Illegible, poor format
Essays   _____ _____   Insufficient Postage
Drawings   _____ _____   Plagarized material
Play   _____ _____   Libelous, lewd or pornographic ma-
Non Fiction   _____   terial
Filler   _____ _____   Critical of government, law agency
                                    or institution
                        _____   Glorifies crime or delinquent conduct
SENT TO: __x__   Deals with criminal technique
                        _____   Offensive to race, nationality, religious
_____   faith, political parties, etc.
_____   _____   Reference to fact writer is an inmate of
_____   State Prison or on Parole therefrom
_____

APPROVED_____ _____
          LIBRARIAN   ASSOC. SUPT. CARE & TREATMENT

AFTERWORD..... ..

GRAVITY DOESN'T REALLY
HAVE MUCH TO DO WITH IT;
THE REASON WE STAY ON
IS THAT THE WORLD

YOU DON'T SAY !